The All About Series

All About ...

Famous Canadians from Prince Edward Island

Barb McDermott and Gail McKeown
Reidmore Books

Reidmore Books Inc.

18228 - 102 Avenue
Edmonton, AB T5S 1S7
phone (780) 444-0912
toll-free 1-800-661-2859
fax (780) 444-0933

website: http://www.reidmore.com
email: reidmore@compusmart.ab.ca

printed and bound in Canada

We acknowledge the financial support of the
Government of Canada through the
Book Publishing Industry Development Program (BPIDP)
for our publishing activities.

Canada

©1999 Reidmore Books

Canadian Cataloguing in Publication Data
McDermott, Barb.
All about famous Canadians from Prince Edward Island

(All about series)
Includes index.
ISBN 1-896132-80-4

1. Prince Edward Island—Biography—Juvenile literature. I. McKeown, Gail.
II. Title. III. Series: McDermott, Barb. All about series.
FC2605.M32 1999 j920.0717   C99-910763-1   F1046.8.M32 1999

About the Authors
Barb McDermott and Gail McKeown are highly experienced
kindergarten teachers living in Ontario. Both hold Bachelor of Arts and
Bachelor of Education degrees, Early Childhood diplomas, specialist
certificates in Primary Education, and have completed qualification
courses in Special Education. As well, Gail has a specialist certificate in
Reading and Visual Arts, and Barb has one in Guidance.

Credits
Editorial: Leah-Ann Lymer, Scott Woodley, David Strand,
Debbie Culbertson
Illustration, design and layout: Bruno Enderlin, Leslieanna Blackner Au
Maps: Wendy Johnson, Johnson Cartographics

Photo Credits
Cover and stamp photo: Lucy Maud Montgomery, from L.M.
Montgomery Collection/Special Collections/University of Guelph Library
Page
3 L.M. Montgomery Collection/Special Collections/University of Guelph
Library
5 L.M. Montgomery Collection/Special Collections/University of Guelph
Library
7 Chris Reardon/Salter Street Films
9 Chris Reardon/Salter Street Films
11 Senator Catherine Callbeck
13 Senator Catherine Callbeck
15 Lennie Gallant
17 Lennie Gallant
19 Mary Hooper
21 Mary Hooper
23 Jann Van Horne/CANAPRESS
25 Rose-Ellen Ghiz
27 Barrett & MacKay Photography Inc.

We have made every effort to identify and credit the sources of
all photographs, illustrations, and information used in this textbook.
Reidmore Books appreciates any further information or corrections;
acknowledgment will be given in subsequent editions.

Table of Contents
(All about what's in the book)

Introduction
(All about the beginning)

People who make the world a better place to live can become famous.

Canada has famous writers, actors, **politicians**, and musicians.

Many famous Canadians are from the **province** of Prince Edward Island.

Gulf of St. Lawrence

PRINCE EDWARD ISLAND

Lucy Maud Montgomery, Clifton

Lennie Gallant, South Rustico

Catherine Callbeck, Central Bedeque

Martha MacIsaac, Charlottetown

Milton Acorn, Charlottetown

Joseph Ghiz, Charlottetown

NEW BRUNSWICK

Northumberland Strait

NOVA SCOTIA

N
W E
S

ARCTIC OCEAN

PACIFIC OCEAN

YUKON

NORTHWEST TERRITORIES

NUNAVUT

BRITISH COLUMBIA

ALBERTA

SASKATCHEWAN

MANITOBA

Hudson Bay

ONTARIO

QUEBEC

NEWFOUNDLAND

ATLANTIC OCEAN

PRINCE EDWARD ISLAND

NOVA SCOTIA

NEW BRUNSWICK

1

Lucy Maud Montgomery (1874-1942)
(All about a famous Canadian writer)

Lucy Maud Montgomery was born in Clifton.

She is 1 of Canada's most popular writers.

Her most famous children's story is Anne of Green Gables.

The main character in Anne of Green Gables is Anne Shirley, who is an **orphan** living in Prince Edward Island.

Lucy Maud Montgomery wrote 7 other books about Anne Shirley, including Anne of Avonlea and Anne's House of Dreams.

Lucy Maud
Montgomery

Lucy Maud Montgomery (1874-1942)
(All about a famous Canadian writer)

Lucy Maud Montgomery was 2 years old when her mother died.

Her father sent her to live with her grandparents near Cavendish.

She wrote stories and poems whenever she was sad.

She worked as a teacher and as a writer for a newspaper called the Daily Echo.

Her stories have been made into movies, plays, and television shows.

Lucy Maud Montgomery Was a Writer and a Teacher

Martha MacIsaac (1986-)
(All about a famous Canadian actor)

Martha MacIsaac was born in Charlottetown.

She is an actor on television.

She plays Emily Starr in the television show called "Emily of New Moon."

"Emily of New Moon" is based on children's stories written by Lucy Maud Montgomery.

The television show is seen in Canada and other countries around the world.

Martha MacIsaac

Martha MacIsaac (1986-)
(All about a famous Canadian actor)

Many children **auditioned** to be Emily in "Emily of New Moon."

One of the producers of the show had seen a picture of Martha MacIsaac in a tourism brochure for Prince Edward Island.

The producer decided that Martha was the girl to play Emily.

Martha enjoys being on the television show so much that she wants to continue to be an actor when she grows up.

Martha MacIsaac Plays Emily Starr

Catherine Callbeck (1939-)
(All about a famous Canadian politician)

Catherine Callbeck was born in Central Bedeque.

She is a politician and a business person.

She is the 1st woman in Canada to be **elected premier.**

She worked for her family business for many years.

The family business was a furniture store and hardware stores.

Catherine Callbeck

11

Catherine Callbeck (1939-)
(All about a famous Canadian politician)

Catherine Callbeck studied at **universities** in Canada and the United States.

She was 1st elected to the provincial government in 1974.

She left politics every few years so that she could work for the family business again.

She was elected premier of Prince Edward Island in 1993.

She became a **senator** in the Senate of Canada in 1997.

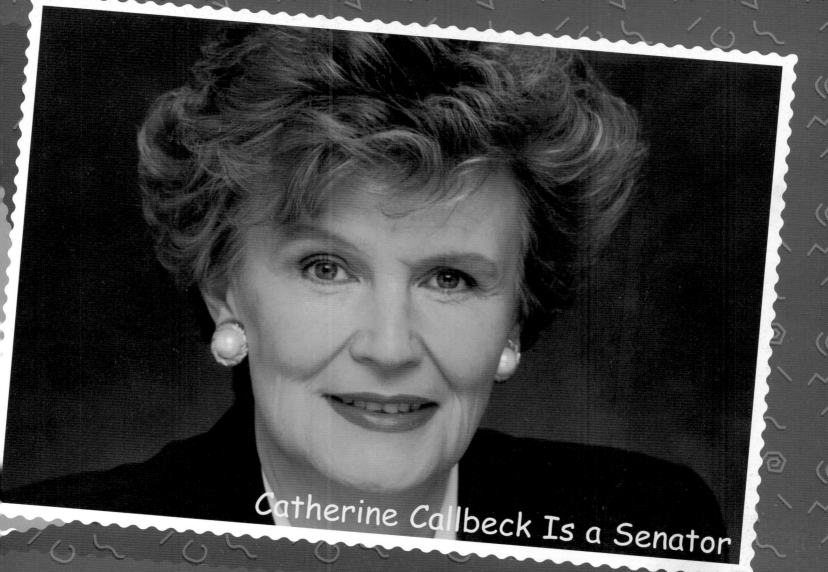

Catherine Callbeck Is a Senator

Lennie Gallant (1955-)
(All about a famous Canadian musician)

Lennie Gallant was born in South Rustico.

He is a singer and song writer.

His albums include *Open Window* and *Lifeline*.

He writes songs in both English and French.

He works with folk, rock, and pop musicians from **Atlantic Canada**.

Lennie Gallant

15

Lennie Gallant (1955-)
(All about a famous Canadian musician)

Many of Lennie Gallant's songs are about life in Atlantic Canada.

He has won awards from the East Coast Music Association.

He has won Song of the Year and Male Artist of the Year awards.

His song called "Which Way Does the River Run" is on an album made by the **United Nations** to celebrate its 50th birthday.

Lennie Gallant Sings About Atlantic Canada

Milton Acorn (1923-1986)
(All about a famous Canadian writer)

Milton Acorn was born in Charlottetown.

He was a writer who wrote 1000s of poems.

Many of his poems are about the lives of working men and women in Canada.

He was named "The People's Poet" by a group of poets in Toronto in 1970.

In 1984 a film called *In Love and Anger* was made about his life.

Milton Acorn

Milton Acorn (1923-1986)
(All about a famous Canadian writer)

Milton Acorn fought and was hurt in World War II.

He moved to Montreal, Quebec after World War II and became a **carpenter**.

He stopped being a carpenter when he published his 1st book of poems in 1956.

His book of poems called *The Island Means Minago* won a Governor General's Award in 1975.

The Milton Acorn People's Poetry Award is named after him and is given each year to an outstanding poet.

Milton Acorn Won Awards

Joseph Ghiz (1945-1996)
(All about a famous Canadian politician)

Joseph Ghiz was born in Charlottetown.

He was a politician and a lawyer.

He was elected premier of Prince Edward Island in 1986.

He became the head of the Dalhousie Law School in Halifax, Nova Scotia in 1995.

He became a **justice** of the Supreme Court of Prince Edward Island in 1995.

Joseph Ghiz

Joseph Ghiz (1945-1996)
(All about a famous Canadian politician)

Joseph Ghiz's father was born in Lebanon in the Middle East.

Joseph Ghiz was the 1st premier of Prince Edward Island whose family did not originally come from **Europe**.

He studied law at universities in Canada and the United States.

He was 1st elected to the provincial government in 1982.

He played an important role in discussions with the **prime minister** and other premiers about the future of Canada.

Joseph Ghiz with Canadian Astronauts

Summary
(All about the ending)

Canada has people who try to make the world a better place to live.

Many famous Canadians are from Prince Edward Island.

Canada has Lucy Maud Montgomery, Martha MacIsaac, Catherine Callbeck, Lennie Gallant, Milton Acorn, and Joseph Ghiz.

Canada has amazing people!

Prince Edward Island Has Amazing People

Glossary
(All about what the words mean)

Atlantic Canada (page 14)
Atlantic means near the Atlantic Ocean. Atlantic Canada is made of the provinces of New Brunswick, Nova Scotia, Prince Edward Island, and Newfoundland.

auditioned (page 8)
To audition is to perform for someone to show him or her your skills. Actors, singers, and dancers audition to get parts in shows.

carpenter (page 20)
A carpenter is a person who builds and repairs things made of wood.

elected (page 10)
A person is elected when he or she has been chosen in a vote.

Europe (page 24)
Europe is an area that includes the countries of France, Italy, Germany, Poland, and the Czech Republic.

justice (page 22)
A justice is a person who tries to decide who is right and who is wrong in court cases.

orphan (page 2)
An orphan is a child whose parents are no longer living.

politicians (page 1)
Politicians are people who have been elected to government, or who are trying to be elected.

premier (page 10)
The premier is the leader of a province's government.

prime minister (page 24)
The prime minister is the leader of Canada's government.

province (page 1)
A province is a separate region in Canada that has its own government.

senator (page 12)
A senator is a member of the Senate of Canada. The Senate is 1 part of the Canadian government.

United Nations (page 16)
The United Nations is an organization of countries that want to help each other and bring peace to the world.

universities (page 12)
Universities are schools that students can go to after they have finished high school.